INSIDE YOUR BODY

ALL ABOUT CHICKENPOX

MEGAN BORGERT-SPANIOL

Consulting Editor, Diane Craig, MA/Reading Specialist

Super Sandcastle

An Imprint of Abdo Publishing
abdopublishing.com

ABDOPUBLISHING.COM

Published by Abdo Publishing, a division of ABDO, PO Box 398166, Minneapolis, Minnesota 55439. Copyright © 2019 by Abdo Consulting Group, Inc. International copyrights reserved in all countries. No part of this book may be reproduced in any form without written permission from the publisher. Super SandCastle™ is a trademark and logo of Abdo Publishing.

Printed in the United States of America,
North Mankato, Minnesota
052018
092018

THIS BOOK CONTAINS
RECYCLED MATERIALS

Design and Production: Mighty Media, Inc.
Editor: Jessie Alkire
Cover Photographs: iStockphoto; Shutterstock
Interior Photographs: iStockphoto; Shutterstock

Library of Congress Control Number: 2017961865

Publisher's Cataloging-in-Publication Data
Names: Borgert-Spaniol, Megan, author.
Title: All about chickenpox / by Megan Borgert-Spaniol.
Description: Minneapolis, Minnesota : Abdo Publishing, 2019. |
    Series: Inside your body set 2
Identifiers: ISBN 9781532115806 (lib.bdg.) | ISBN 9781532156526
    (ebook)
Subjects: LCSH: Human body--Juvenile literature. | Chickenpox--
    Juvenile literature. | Childhood diseases--Juvenile literature. |
Communicable diseases--Juvenile literature.
Classification: DDC 616.914--dc23

CONTENTS

YOUR BODY	4
ALL ABOUT CHICKENPOX	6
CAUSES	8
SIGNS AND SYMPTOMS	10
ITCHING AND SCRATCHING	12
CONTAGIOUS!	14
SHINGLES	16
TREATMENT	18
MEDICINES AND REMEDIES	20
PREVENTION	22
GLOSSARY	24

YOUR BODY

AREAS AFFECTED BY CHICKENPOX

You're amazing! So is your body.
Most of the time your body works just fine.
It lets you go to school, play with friends,
and more. But sometimes you feel sick or
part of you hurts.

4

Chickenpox is a common illness affecting kids. It makes you feel sick and **itchy**. Most people who get chickenpox only get it once. Others are vaccinated against chickenpox. They usually don't get it at all!

HAVE YOU EVER HAD CHICKENPOX?

ALL ABOUT
CHICKENPOX

Chickenpox is an **infection**. It often feels like a cold or the flu. Most people get chickenpox during childhood. After that, they are immune to it. This means they usually won't get chickenpox again.

Chickenpox causes a **rash**. It is **itchy**! It looks like spots on the skin. The spots first appear on the belly, back, or face. Then the rash spreads to the rest of the body.

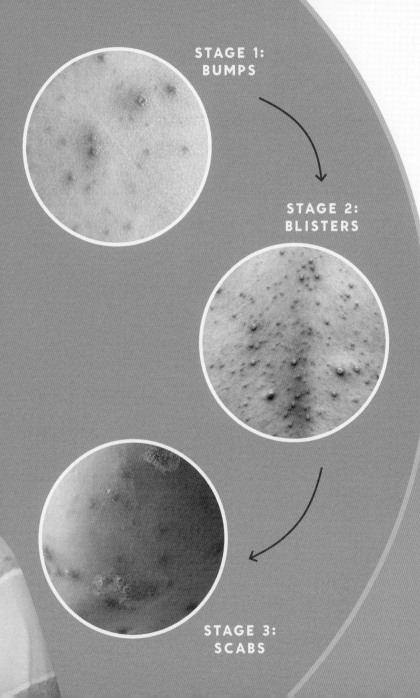

STAGE 1:
BUMPS

STAGE 2:
BLISTERS

STAGE 3:
SCABS

Chickenpox spots have three stages.

STAGE 1: BUMPS

Raised pink or red bumps appear on the skin.

STAGE 2: BLISTERS

The bumps turn into **blisters**. They are filled with liquid. The blisters break after a day or two.

STAGE 3: SCABS

The broken blisters crust over into scabs.

New bumps break out over several days. That means all three stages of spots appear on the body at the same time.

CAUSES

Chickenpox is caused by a virus. It is called *varicella zoster*. The virus can spread through the air. It can also spread through contact with **mucus**, **saliva**, or **blister** liquid.

Certain people are more likely to get chickenpox. Do any of these describe you? If so, you may be more likely to get chickenpox!

HAVE NOT YET HAD CHICKENPOX

HAVE NOT BEEN VACCINATED AGAINST CHICKENPOX

GO TO A SCHOOL WITH OTHER KIDS

LIVE WITH
OTHER CHILDREN

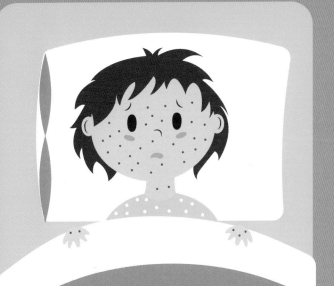

SIGNS
AND SYMPTOMS

Early chickenpox **symptoms** can feel like a cold or flu. After a day or two, spots begin to appear. It takes five to ten days for all the spots to become scabs.

Common Chickenpox Symptoms

HEADACHE

STOMACHACHE

LOSS OF APPETITE

ITCHY RASH

FEVER

TIREDNESS

Spot Count

Some kids with chickenpox have only a few spots.
Others have hundreds from head to toe!

ITCHING
AND SCRATCHING

Chickenpox is an uncomfortable illness. When your spots become **blisters**, they start to feel **itchy**. But don't scratch your spots!

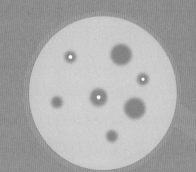

Scratching can tear your skin. This will leave scars when the blisters heal.

Scratching also spreads **germs**. Your blisters can become **infected** with bacteria.

There are many things you can do to keep from scratching.

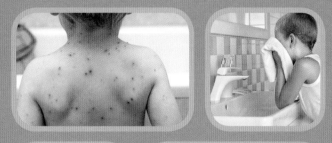

Stay Cool

Soothe **itchy** skin with cool baths or ice packs.

Pat, Don't Rub

Softly pat your body dry with a towel after bathing.

Trim Your Fingernails

This protects your skin if you scratch.

Wash Your Hands

This stops the spread of **germs**.

Stay Busy!

Keep your mind off scratching by coloring, reading, or doing other activities.

CONTAGIOUS!

The chickenpox virus is highly contagious. This means it is easily passed from person to person. There are several ways the virus can spread.

COUGHING

SNEEZING

SKIN CONTACT

CONTACT WITH BLISTER LIQUID

SHARING CUPS, SPOONS, OR FORKS

Rash

By the time your **rash** appears, you are already contagious. That means you may have spread the virus without knowing it! This is often how kids with chickenpox **infect** others.

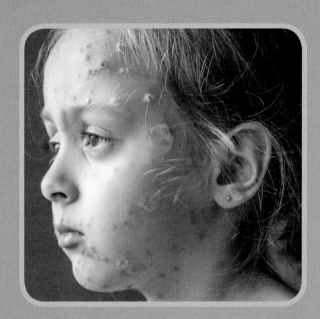

Blisters

If you have chickenpox, you are contagious until your **blisters** turn into scabs. You should stay home from school until then.

SHINGLES

After you get chickenpox, the virus stays in your body. The virus might remain inactive for the rest of your life. But the virus can become active months or years later. It causes an **infection** called shingles.

Shingles **symptoms** are similar to chickenpox symptoms.

HEADACHE

FEVER

TIREDNESS

SKIN TINGLING, ITCHING, OR PAIN

RASH OF RED BUMPS AND BLISTERS

For healthy people, most shingles cases are mild. But shingles can sometimes lead to **complications**.

Shingles Complications

• pain caused by harmed nerves

• vision loss

• skin **infections**

• facial **paralysis**

Shingles usually goes away on its own. But you should still call your doctor if you think you have shingles. He may give you medicines to help you heal.

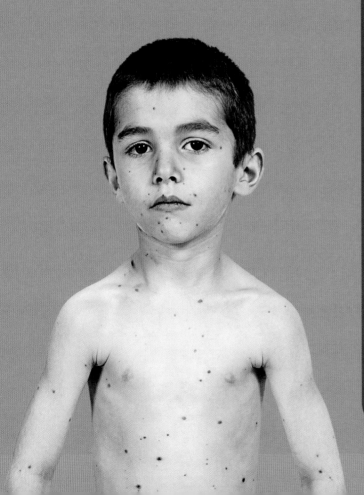

TREATMENT

Most cases of chickenpox heal with time and rest. But your doctor may recommend medicines too.

Antiviral medicines can lessen the effects of chickenpox.

Antibiotics treat **blisters** that are **infected** by bacteria.

Antihistamines help relieve **itching**.

When to Call

Chickenpox can lead to **complications**. Call your doctor right away if you have more severe **symptoms**.

- Trouble breathing

- Stiff neck

- **Rash** that is warm, swollen, or sore

- Rash that spreads to your eyes

- Vomiting

- Dizziness

- Confusion

- Tiredness

- Fever that rises above 102 degrees Fahrenheit (38.9°C)

MEDICINES
AND REMEDIES

Chickenpox takes time to heal. But there are medicines to make you feel more comfortable. Ask your doctor before you take any medicine for chickenpox **symptoms**.

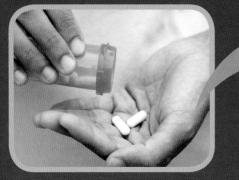

ACETAMINOPHEN
(ah-seet-a-MEN-oh-fin)

a medicine that helps reduce pain and fever

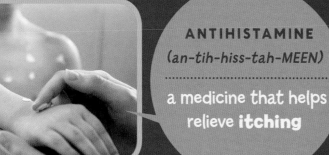

ANTIHISTAMINE
(an-tih-hiss-tah-MEEN)

a medicine that helps relieve **itching**

WARNING

Do NOT take aspirin if you have chickenpox. This can lead to a serious condition called Reye's syndrome. It causes swelling in the liver and brain.

NATURAL REMEDIES

You can also help ease pain and **itching** with remedies at home.

CALAMINE LOTION

Apply calamine lotion to your spots.

COOL, SOFT FOOD

Eat cool, soft foods if you have **blisters** in your mouth.

BAKING SODA AND OATMEAL

Add baking soda or finely ground oatmeal to your bath.

PREVENTION

The best way to prevent chickenpox is by getting the vaccine. Most people who are vaccinated will not get chickenpox. Those who do get chickenpox will usually have milder **symptoms**.

The chickenpox vaccine is a shot. It gives you a small dose of the chickenpox virus. Then your body makes **antibodies** to fight the virus. This helps you become immune to the virus.

Doctors recommend the chickenpox vaccine to certain groups.

YOUNG CHILDREN

OLDER CHILDREN WHO HAVE
NOT HAD CHICKENPOX

ADULTS WHO HAVE NOT HAD
CHICKENPOX BUT MAY BE
EXPOSED TO THE VIRUS

If you have had
chickenpox,
you don't need to
be vaccinated.

ANTIBODY- a substance produced by the body to fight an attack.

BLISTER - a bubble filled with fluid on the skin.

COMPLICATION - a second condition that develops during the course of a primary disease or condition.

GERM - a tiny, living organism that can make people sick.

INFECT - to cause sickness by spreading bacteria or other germs. Such a sickness is an infection.

ITCH - feeling irritated or bothersome.

MUCUS - a slippery, sticky substance produced by the body.

PARALYSIS - the loss of motion or feeling in a part of the body.

RASH - a breaking out of red spots on the skin.

SALIVA - a liquid produced in the mouth.

SYMPTOM - a noticeable change in the normal working of the body.

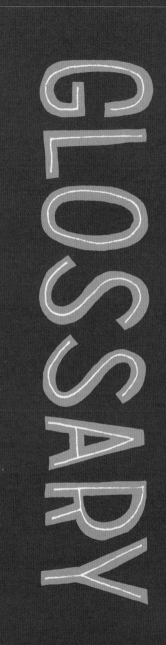

GLOSSARY